Play and Learn
by Karen O'Callaghan

Illustrated by Linda Worrall, Steve Ling and Phil Weare

Cover design by Oxprint Ltd

Edited by Debbie Lines

ISBN 0 86112 596 7
© Brimax Books Ltd 1990. All rights reserved.
Published by Brimax Books, Newmarket, England 1990.
Printed in Spain by Graficromo S.A., Cordoba.

PLAY and LEARN

Brimax Books · Newmarket · England

Let's Learn our ABC

This book is designed to be more than an alphabet. Each page offers opportunities to extend the child's awareness, knowledge and vocabulary. The illustrations for each letter of the alphabet are based on actions and combined with descriptive text which introduces other concepts such as, big/little, up/down, rough/smooth.

The letter is printed in **bold** where it appears in the text. This helps to focus the child's attention on the letter and its position, clearly showing that it is not always an initial sound but may appear in the middle or at the end of different words.

Within schools the sound a letter makes is taught before the letter name, as this is an important function of word building.

An adult reading with a child can lay emphasis on the sound of each letter. Extra learning is possible by an adult discussing alternative words that begin with the same sound and adding to the examples given. The two children illustrated, are seen co-operating with and helping each other in everyday situations which can be easily recognised and which enable children to copy the actions and go through the pages by themselves. This can make learning fun.

Alex is looking **all** around for Zoe.
"Here I **a**m, **A**lex!" says Zoe.

Point to **all** the **Aa**'s.

Bb

Blow a piece of paper across the floor.
Bend down low and **b**low, **b**low, **b**low!

Where are the **Bb**'s?

Curl up tight. Alex and Zoe make themselves small.
Can you **c**url up, too?

Can you see the **Cc**'s?

Dd

Dancing is fun! You can **d**o it, too! Alex **d**ances with te**dd**y. Zoe makes the **d**oll **d**ance as well!

12

Where are the Dd's?

Eating ic**e** cr**e**am.
Al**e**x is still **e**ating his ic**e** cream.
"Min**e**'s all gon**e**," says Zo**e**.

Can you se**e th**e** **Ee**'s?**

Ff

Finding the best way.
"These won't **f**it in," says Alex.
"**If** we **f**old them they will **f**it,"
says Zoe.

"Folding makes things smaller."
Fold a piece of paper.
Does it get smaller?

Find all the Ff's.

Gg

"**G**o on Zoe, open it!" says Alex.
Who is **g**ivin**g** a present?
Who is **g**ettin**g** a present?

16

Where are all the **Gg**'s?

You deserve the best.

So, let us give you a complimentary issue of the *new Mirabella*!

Smart. Sexy. Savvy. Fun. The *new* **Mirabella** is the essence of today's sophisticated woman—each issue is overflowing with fresh, modern ideas on fashion, beauty and on your way of life. Fuel your imagination, spark your interests and enrich your sense of style. Send for your free issue today!

☐ **YES!** Send me my free issue of the *new* **Mirabella** immediately! If I'm delighted, I'll receive 5 more issues (for a total of 6 issues–1 year) and be billed for $9.97. If not, I'll write "cancel" on my bill and owe nothing. But the free issue is mine to keep!

Name _____ 42A2

Address _____

City _____

State _____ Zip _____

FREE ISSUE!

☐ Enter my 1-year (12 issues) subscription to ELLE for $26.00

Canadian orders add $10 per year (includes 7% GST); foreign orders add $10 per year; payment in U.S. funds must accompany order. Please allow 30 to 60 days for delivery of first issue.

Would you like to receive special offers from qualified users of our mailing list? ☐ Yes ☐ No

BUSINESS REPLY MAIL

FIRST CLASS MAIL   PERMIT NO. 1257   BOULDER, CO

POSTAGE WILL BE PAID BY ADDRESSEE

Mirabella ®

P.O. BOX 55251
BOULDER CO 80323-5251

Here is Alex **h**olding a bucket.
Zoe is **h**elping **h**im to fill it wit**h** sand.

Hh

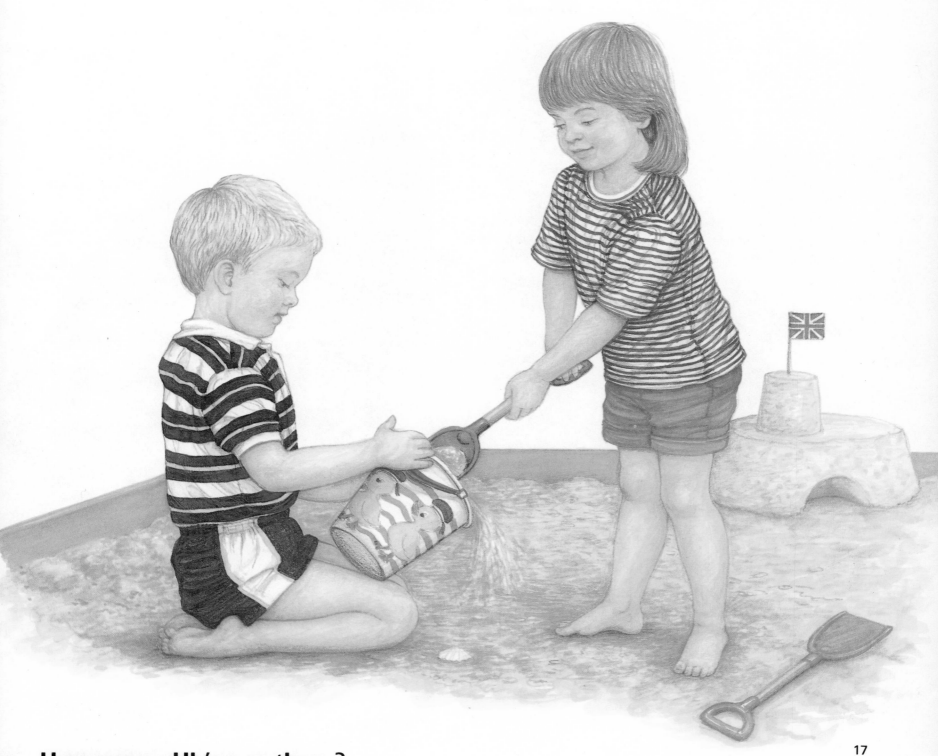

How many **Hh**'s are there?

Ii

"I am **inside** our tent," says Zoe.
"I am **inside it**, too," says Alex.

Find the **Ii**'s.

Join in a jumping game!
Jump, jump, as high as you can.

Point to the **Jj**'s.

Kk

Kic**k** a ball as hard as you can, see how far it goes!
Loo**k**, Alex **k**ic**k**s the leaves up in the air and everywhere.

20

Look for all the **Kk**'s.

Look at Alex, he is trying to lift
the bricks all at once.
Zoe can't do it – she is laughing
too much!

Look for all the Ll's.

Mm

Moving about.
"When I **m**ove, **m**y shadow **m**oves with **m**e," says Alex.

"I can see **m**yself in the **m**irror," says Zoe.

Mm

How **m**any **Mm**'s can you find?

Nn

Nod your head up and down
to mean 'yes'.
Now shake your head from side
to side to mean 'no'.

Point to the **Nn**'s

"**O**ver the chairs we g**o**!" says Z**o**e.
Z**o**e and Alex climb **o**n –
and jump **o**ff!

O o

Point to the **Oo**'s.

25

Pp

"**P**lease hel**p** me, Zoe. We can move this together! I'll **p**ush," says Alex. "I'll **p**ull," says Zoe.

Point to the **Pp**'s.

Quiet! Shh! Shh! Sit **q**uietly.
What can you hear when you are
sitting **q**uietly?

Qq

Where are the Qq's?

Rr

Run, run as fast as you can.
Round and **round** and **round!**

Find the **Rr**'s.

See us **s**haring a picnic.
"**S**ome cookie**s** for you
and a **s**andwich for me."

Ss

Spot the **Ss**'s.

Tt

Touch something rough like **t**ree bark. Look for something smoo**t**h **t**o **t**ouch like flower pe**t**als.

Touch all the Tt's.

"**U**nder we go!"
Yo**u** m**u**st make yo**u**rself flat
to go **u**nder the table.

Can you** find the **Uu**'s?**

Vv

Visiting is fun! Zoe and Alex **v**isit their friend.
He is **v**ery pleased to see them.

Point to the **Vv**'s.

Ww

Walking **tw**o **w**ays!
Walk **w**ith great big steps.
Walk **w**ith tiny little steps.

Where are the **Ww**'s?

It's exciting making **X**'s!
Make yourself look like an **X**.
Make e**x**tra **X**'s with your legs
and fingers.

Spot the Xx's.

Yy

"You're yawning, Alex." says Zoe.
"I can see you!"

"I'm not tired," says Alex.
"Come and play."

How many **Yy**'s can **y**ou see?

Zoe and Alex are following a **z**ig**z**ag path down the mountain.

Point to each letter **Zz**.

We can count

We Can Count 123

These pages are designed to encourage children to observe and count objects within their own environment.

Counting Our Toys from 1–10 is the basic section. Each page shows the number as a symbol, a numeral and a written word – three ways to explain simply to a child the number concept. Colours are also introduced.

Counting at Home/Outside/In the Supermarket – These are familiar situations for children everywhere which stimulate their interest. The child is invited to join in, to find and count using the illustrated number/picture/ word key. Repetition of this concept can be used by parents to help children count the numerous objects they can see around them.

The ideas are expanded further to include the order and grouping of numbers, counting backwards, and to show the various activities and games your child can follow.

All children love rhymes. The number rhymes provide a fun way to establish solid and basic number concepts.

Given the examples in these pages, parents can develop new games with their children which involve numbers and counting.

Learning numbers can be great fun.

Alex and Zoe
are counting their toys.
Turn the pages and you can count too.

one rocking horse

•	1	**one**

two bicycles

••	2	**two**

three boats

| • • • | 3 | **three** |

four teddy bears

| :: | 4 | **four** |

five dolls

| :·: | 5 | **five** |

six balls

| :·: :·: :·: | 6 | **six** |

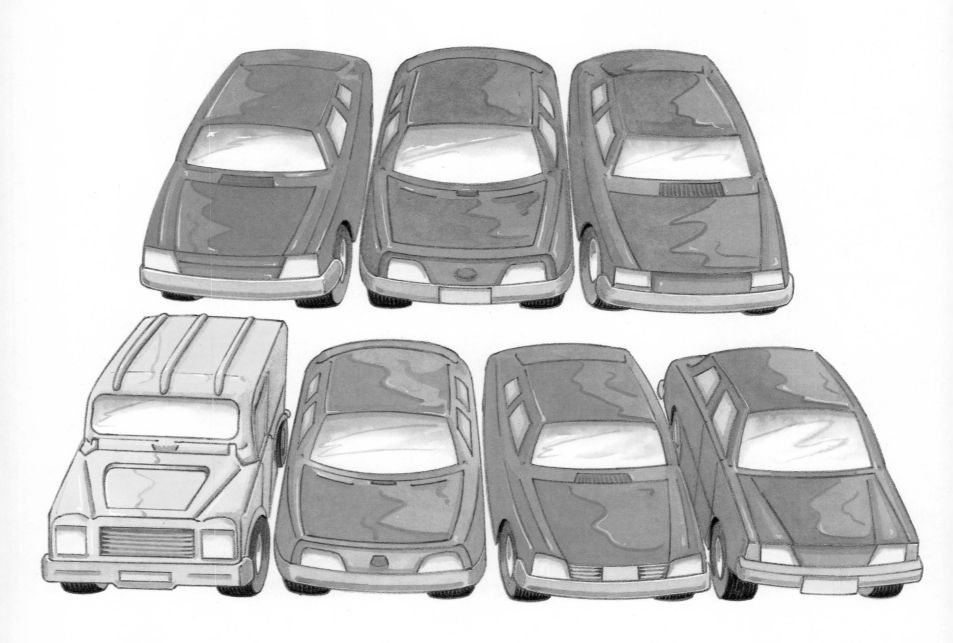

seven cars

⠿	7	**seven**

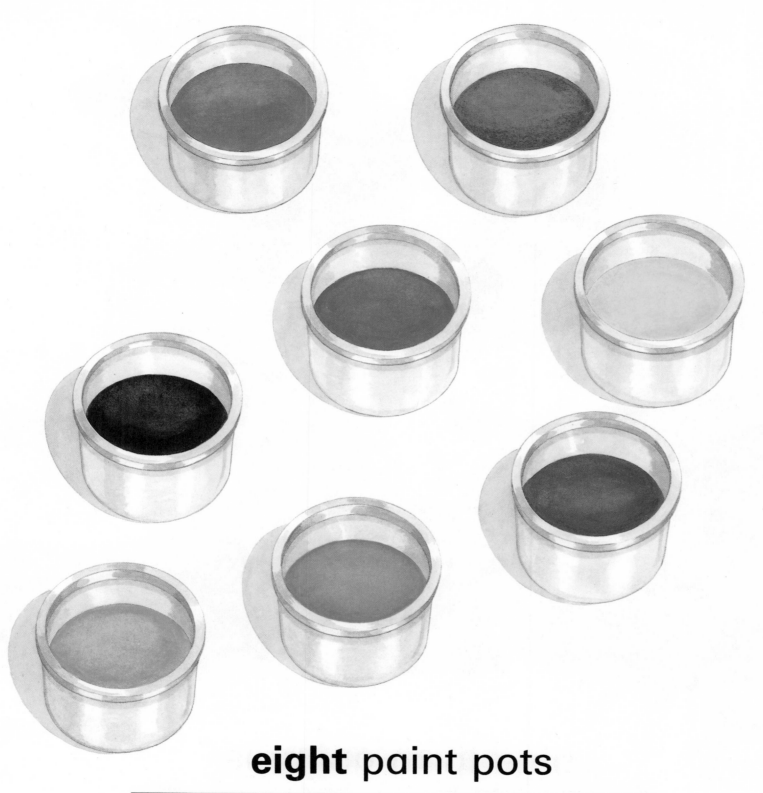

eight paint pots

| ⠿⠿ | 8 | **eight** |

nine farm animals

:::::·:	9	**nine**

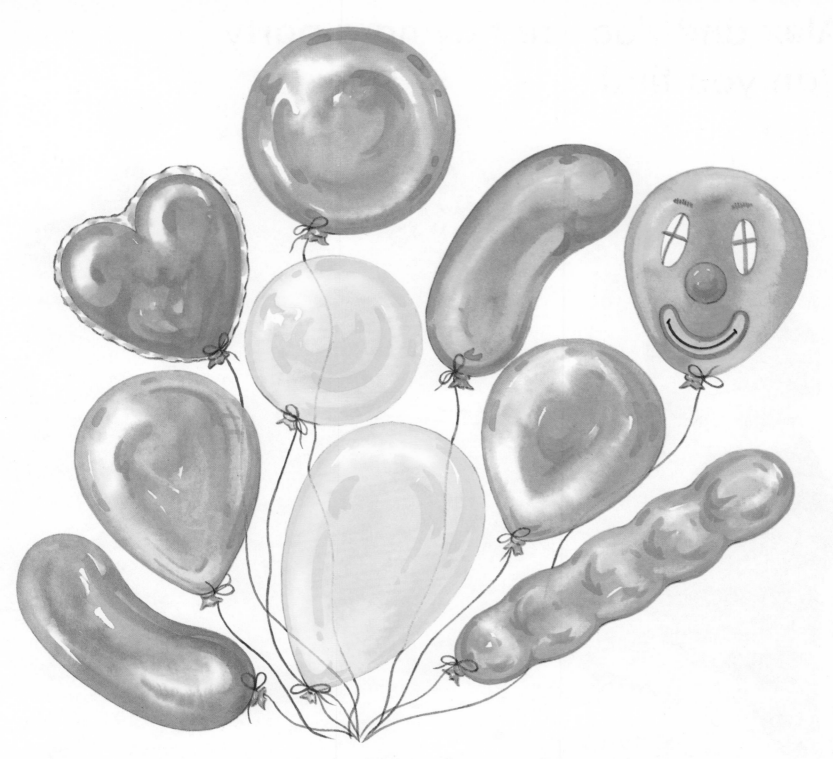

ten balloons

| :::::::::: | 10 | **ten** |

Alex and Zoe are having a party.
Can you find . . .?

1		cake
2		jugs
3		bowls
4		glasses
5		spoons
6		candles
7		plates
8		straws
9		buns
10		cookies

Counting outside
Can you find . . .?

56

1		church
2		buses
3		trucks
4		bicycles
5		cars
6		street lights
7		birds
8		houses
9		trees
10		people

Counting in the supermarket
Find and count with us . . .

1		chicken
2		loaves
3		cartons of milk
4		packets of butter
5		cans of beans
6		eggs
7		yoghurts
8		oranges
9		tomatoes
10		burgers

We can make a number stairway with bricks. Can you?

Count with us to the top and back down again.

Counting backwards

"Help me with the countdown," says Zoe. "Are you ready?"

6

7

8

9

10

"We have lift off!" says Alex.
"We are off to the moon."

0

1

2

3

4

5

63

Let's make a long train.

1st   2nd   3rd 4th   5th

"I am first, I am the driver," says Zoe.

6th   7th   8th   9th   10th

"I am last, I am the guard," says Alex.

We are sorting our toys.
We can put our bricks

in 5's

in 2's

in 4's

in 3's

Alex has sorted the toys into . . .

2	![shovel and flashlight]	blue
3	![ball, block, car]	green
4	![book, duck, wagon, truck]	yellow
5	![boat, truck, bucket, car, plane]	red

67

Zoe has put together . . .

2		planes
3		cars
4		boats
5		balls

Join in our counting rhyme

There were **10** in the bed . . .

And the little one said,
"Roll over, roll over!"
So they all rolled over
And one fell out.

There were **9** in the bed . . .

And the little one said,
"Roll over, roll over!"
So they all rolled over
And one fell out.

There were **8** in the bed . . .

And the little one said,
"Roll over, roll over!"
So they all rolled over
And one fell out.

There were **7** in the bed . . .

And the little one said,
"Roll over, roll over!"
So they all rolled over
And one fell out.

There were **6** in the bed . . .

And the little one said,
"Roll over, roll over!"
So they all rolled over
And one fell out.

There were **5** in the bed . . .

And the little one said,
"Roll over, roll over!"
So they all rolled over
And one fell out.

There were **4** in the bed . . .

And the little one said,
"Roll over, roll over!"
So they all rolled over
And one fell out.

There were **3** in the bed . . .

And the little one said,
"Roll over, roll over!"
So they all rolled over
And one fell out.

There were **2** in the bed . . .
And the little one said,
"Roll over, roll over!"
So they both rolled over
And one fell out.

There was **1** in the bed . . .
And the little one said,
"Roll over, roll over!"
So she rolled over
And she fell out.

There were none in the bed
And no one said,
"Roll over, roll over!"
"We are all down here!"
How many on the floor?

Say this counting rhyme with us

One red engine puffing down the track
One red engine puffing puffing back.

Two blue engines puffing down the trac
Two blue engines puffing puffing back.

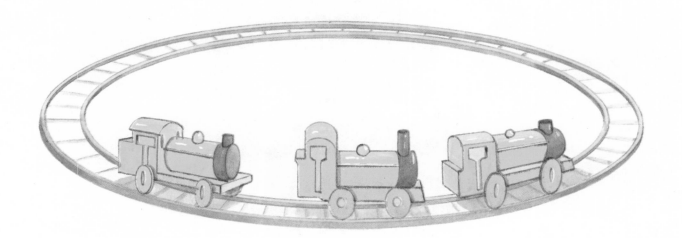

Three yellow engines puffing down the track
Three yellow engines puffing puffing back.

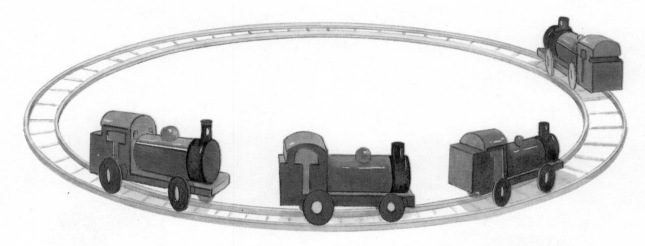

Four green engines puffing down the track
Four green engines puffing puffing back.

Five orange engines puffing down the track
Five orange engines puffing puffing back.

We can read Words

We Can Read Words

This book provides a valuable aid and guide to enable children to describe their own experiences and the world around them by using words and pictures. The pictures help children to use words, even if at first they cannot read them.

The first section is alphabetically presented to help make word-finding easier. It also contains subjects that a child might see, draw and subsequently want to write about. The following sections show the child, in easy stages, how to begin to write by using simple linking and descriptive words. There are characters in stories; games to play; the weather; jobs people do, etc.

The book will help to extend vocabulary, develop writing skills and imagination. It will open up the exciting world of the written language at any stage of early learning. Children will return to this book again and again to discover new words and the fun of creative writing by themselves.

Looking for words

"How can I write 'house'?" says Zoe.
"I will turn the pages and look for 'h'," says Alex.

A a

airport

alligator

ambulance

ant

apple

astronaut

B b

ball

bed

bicycle

bird

boat

bus

cake

castle

cat

clown

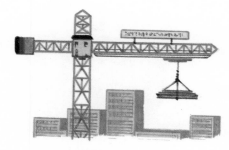

crane

crown

dinosaur

dog

doll

donkey

drum

duck

E e

eagle

egg

elephant

emu

envelope

eskimo

F f

fire truck

fish

flag

flowers

frog

fruit

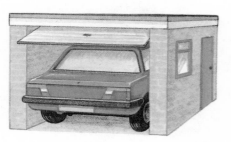
garage

garden

giraffe

gloves

gorilla

grapes

hammer

hamster

helicopter

horse

hospital

house

I i

ice cream

igloo

Indian

insect

iron

island

J j

jaguar

jeans

jellyfish

jet plane

jigsaw

jug

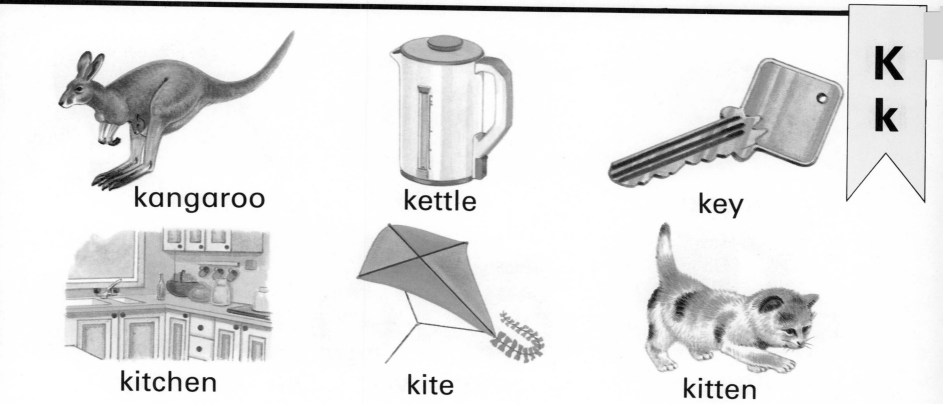

kangaroo

kettle

key

kitchen

kite

kitten

ladybird

leaves

lemon

lighthouse

lion

lollipop

M m

mask

milk

monkey

moon

motorcycle

mouse

N n

necklace

nest

net

newspaper

night

nuts

octopus

onion

orange

ostrich

oven

owl

parachute

party

picnic

pig

pirate

puppet

Q q

quail

quarter

queen

queue

quill

quilt

R r

rabbit

racing car

radio

robin

rocket

rose

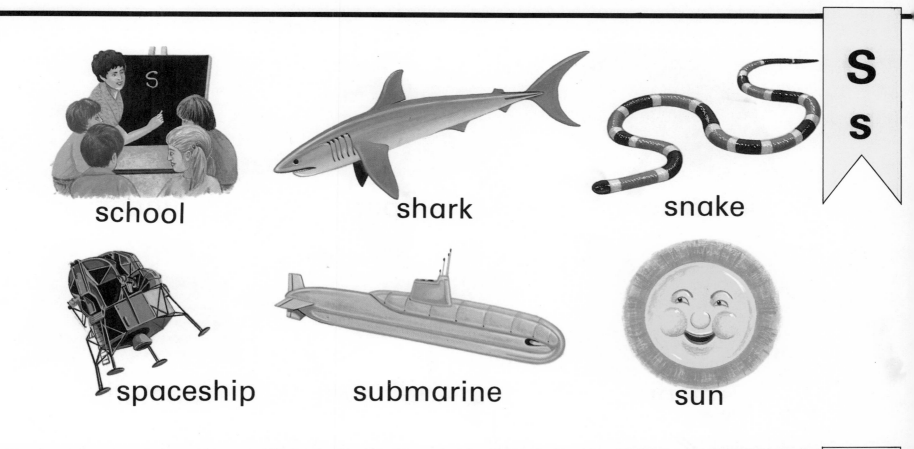

school   shark   snake

spaceship   submarine   sun

S s

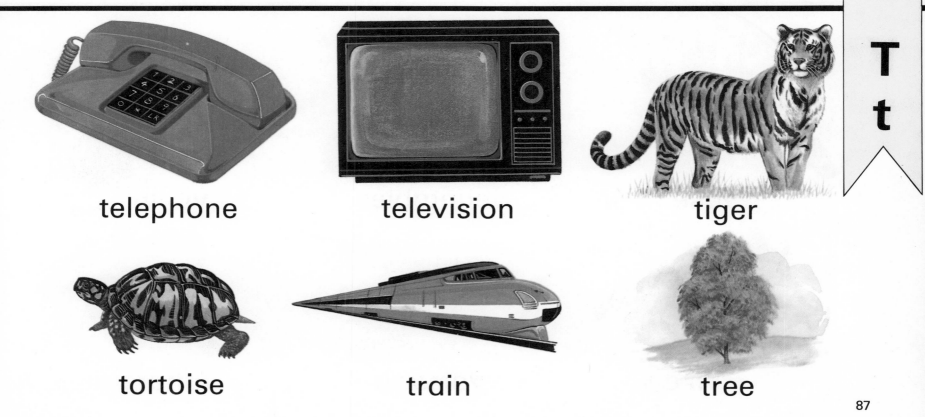

telephone   television   tiger

tortoise   train   tree

T t

U u

umbrella

umpire

under

unicorn

upside down

upstairs

V v

vase

vegetables

violin

vixen

volcano

vulture

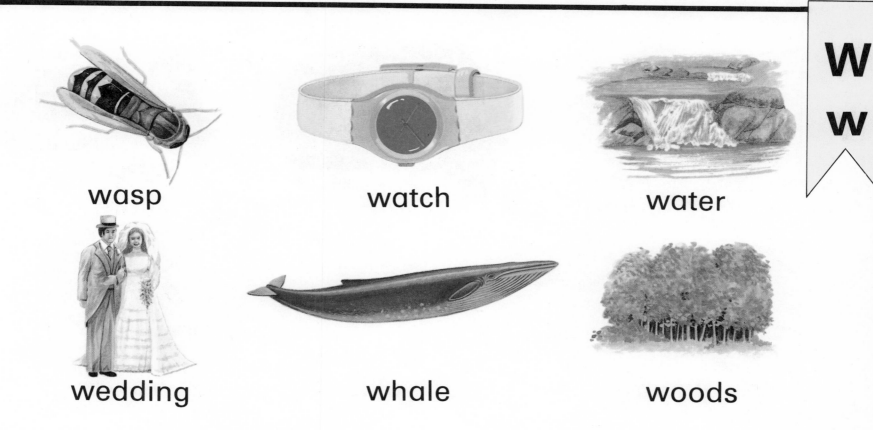

wasp

watch

water

wedding

whale

woods

x-ray

xylophone

axe

boxer

fox

box

Y y

yacht

yak

yard

yawn

yolk

yo-yo

Z z

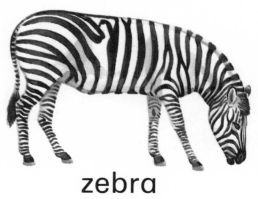
zebra

zig-zag

zipper

zoo

Alex writes house.
"Now I will write about
my house," says Alex.

Ways to begin to write

Here is a . . . .

This is my . . . .

I can see . . . .

I went to . . . .

First draw a picture.
Choose one line on this page to begin writing.
Look for other words you need in the pages of this book.

Little words we can use

it	me	at	up
is	my	an	he
on	we	am	do
to	us	go	if

and	had	she	out
the	saw	you	new
are	his	get	fun
has	her	for	our

they	like	into	look
make	made	with	help
went	dear	love	from
some	down	said	none

Ways to start a story

Once upon a time there was . . . .

Long long ago there lived . . . .

One day . . . .

In the land of . . . .

First draw a picture.
Choose one line on this page to begin your story.
Look for other words you need in the pages of this book.

Characters in a story

king

queen

prince

princess

wizard

witch

ghost

giant

dragon

fairy

mermaid

elf

Opposites

The car is fast.

The tortoise is slow.

big   little   fat   thin

old   new   hot   cold

in   out   happy   sad

Things we can do . . .

We like this game.

It is fun.

We take turns to throw the hoops at the target.

hop

skip

jump

run

draw

write

paint

read

make

dig

catch

ride

Places to go . . .

We like to go to the beach.

We can play on the beach with our friends.

We can make sandcastles.

library

park

playground

farm

zoo

fair

The weather

It has been raining.

We put on our raincoats and boots

and splash in the puddles.

snowing

foggy

sunny

windy

frosty

stormy

People we know

We can play a game.

Alex is the doctor.

Zoe is the nurse.

Teddy is ill. We can make him better.

fireman

teacher

painter

farmer

dentist

builder

Which day is it?

Yesterday was . . .
Today is . . .
Tomorrow will be . . .

In one day we . . .

get up

wash

dress

eat

work

play

help

undress

bath

watch

go to bed

sleep

Let's look at Animals

Let's Look at Animals

Animals are a fascinating part of our world. In these pages, children can discover and learn about domestic, wild, rare and exotic species depicted in their natural surroundings.

In the first section are shown familiar pets, followed by animals found in the garden, on the seashore and on the farm. These are places known to many children where they are able to come into close contact with animals. They can touch, watch and form relationships with them.

Wild animals are less accessible. The last section introduces them grouped according to their own environment – woodland, forest, grassland, desert, jungle and cold lands.

The illustrations provide a realistic view of more than a hundred living creatures, what they look like; where and how they live.

The simply worded text conveys a wealth of interesting facts about animals at an easy reading level.

Alex and Zoe are looking at pets

puppy

kitten

112 rabbit

guinea pig

hamster

goldfish

budgerigar

tortoise

In the garden

butterfly

sparrow

woodlice

spider

ladybirds

caterpillars

ants

earwigs

114

worms

snails

The snail has a round shell.
It moves slowly across the garden.

The sparrow is looking for food.
It likes to eat insects.

On the seashore

seagulls

starfish

limpets

anemones

hermit crab

sea urchin

mussels

crabs

periwinkles

whelks

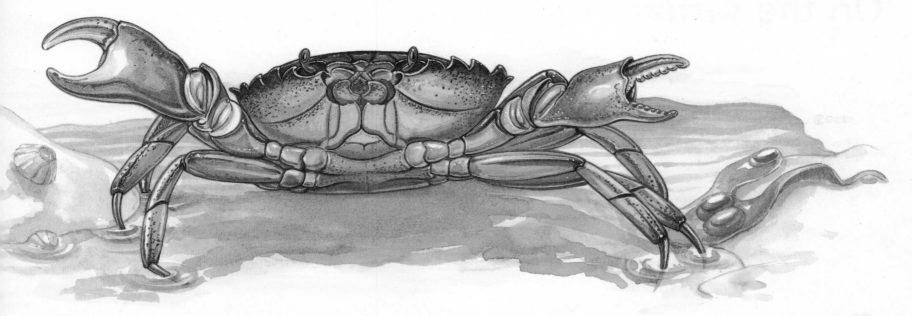

This crab has two big claws.
It walks sideways across the sand.

Seagulls live in nests on cliffs.
They fly over the seashore looking for
fish to eat.

On the farm

sheep

horse

cow

donkey

hens

Cows give us milk to drink.

We get wool from sheep.

hen

chick

cockerel

mare

foal

stallion

cow

calf

bull

drake

duck

duckling

ram

lamb

ewe

boar

sow

piglet

These animals live with people.
They are tame.

giraffe

polar bear

elephant

These animals live free all over
the world. They are wild.

In the forest

black bear

raccoon

porcupine

rattlesnake

chipmunk

woodpecker

skunk

beaver

125

Black bear cubs are good at climbing trees.

Beavers use their strong teeth to chop down trees to make their home.

This porcupine climbs trees to feed
on buds, twigs and bark.

Rattlesnakes are poisonous. They use
the rattles at the end of their tails
to warn away enemies.

In the grassland

lion

elephant

gazelle

cheetah

vulture

giraffe

rhinoceros

zebra

ostrich

hyena

129

The cheetah is the fastest animal
on land.

Giraffes eat leaves at the top of trees.
They pull the leaves off using their tongues.

Ostriches can run very fast on their long legs.

Elephants cool themselves
in the water. They squirt water
with their trunks.

In the desert

elf owl

jack rabbit

gila monster

roadrunner

chuckwalla

kangaroo rat

sidewinder

133

The gila monster is a poisonous
lizard. It moves slowly in the hot sun.

The jack rabbit has big ears
to help it stay cool.

The roadrunner can run better than it can fly.

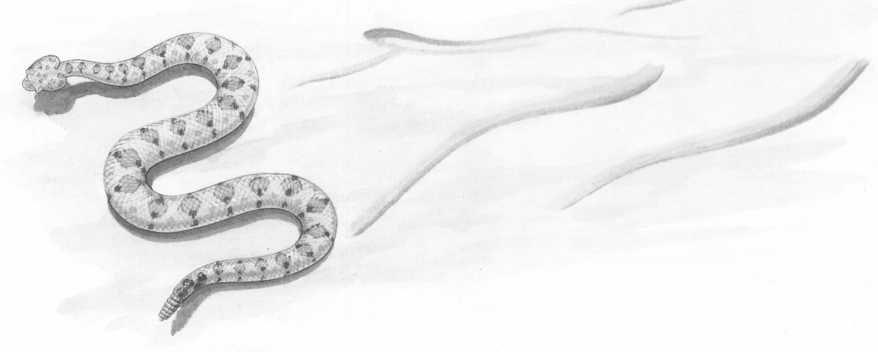

The sidewinder moves its body sideways across the sand.

In the jungle

parrot

chameleon

gorilla

leopard

chimpanzee

mandrill

frog

137

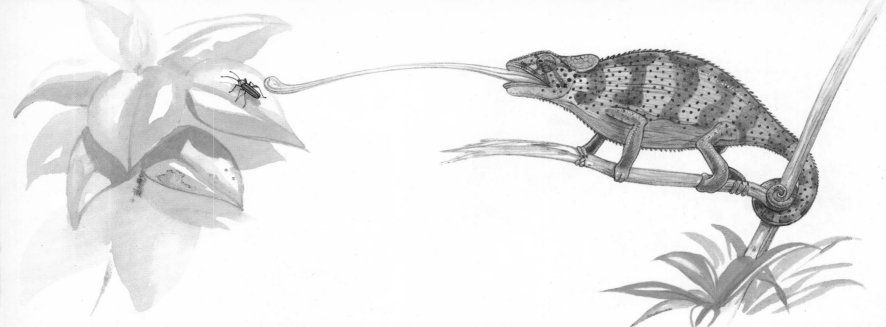

Chameleons live in trees. This one is
using its long tongue to catch food.

Chimpanzees do not drink very often.
When they do they dip their hands
into the water then lick them.

The grey parrot eats seeds and nuts.
It can copy the calls of other birds.

Gorillas are big and strong.
They are also quiet and gentle.

In the cold lands

musk ox

grey wolf

arctic fox

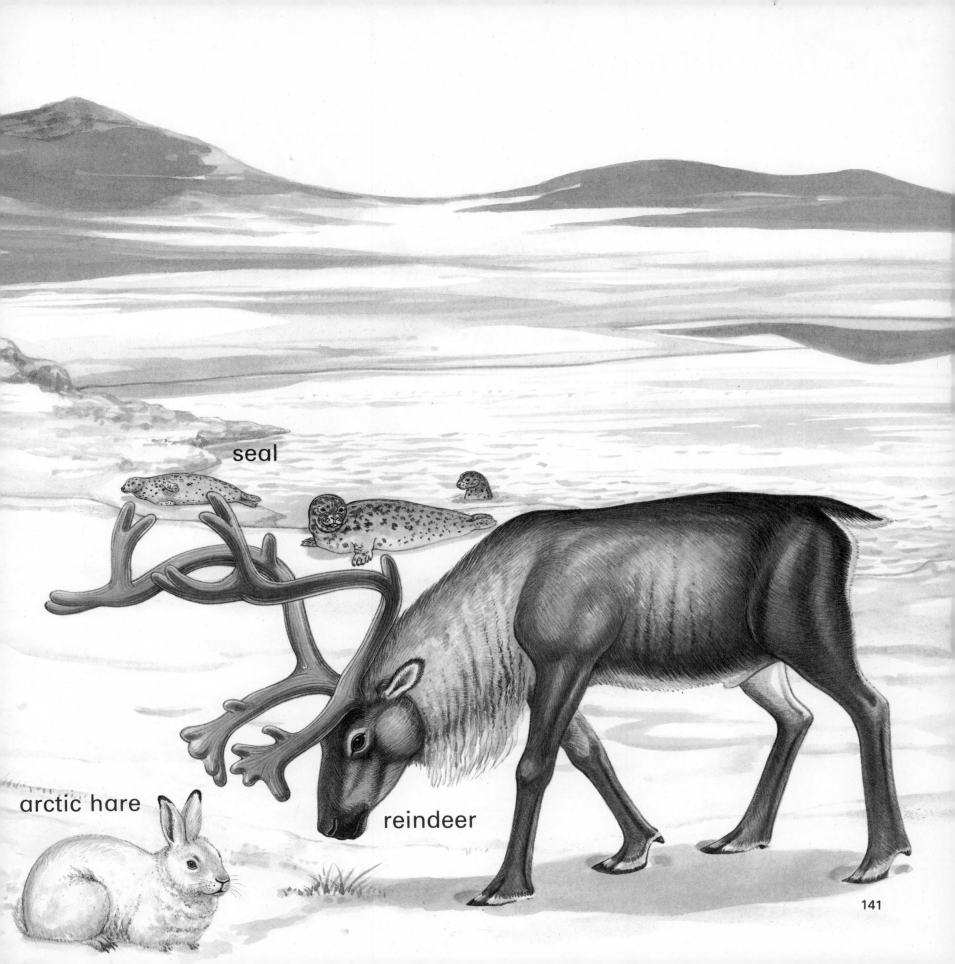

seal

arctic hare

reindeer